1. Prologue

THERE is perhaps nothing extraordinary in the fact that man is wise and just, takes great care to provide for his own children, -shows due consideration for his parents, seeks sustenance for himself, protects himself against plots, and possesses all the other gifts of nature which are his. For man has been endowed with speech, of all things the most precious, and has been granted reason, which is of the greatest help and use.

Moreover, he knows how to reverence and worship the gods. But that dumb animals should by nature possess some good quality and should have many of man's amazing excellences assigned to them along with man, is indeed a remarkable fact. And to know accurately the special characteristics of each, and how living creatures also have been a source of interest no less than man, demands a trained intelligence and much learning. Now I am well aware of the labour that others have expended on this subject, yet I have collected all the materials that I could; I have clothed them in untechnical language, and am persuaded that my achievement is a treasure far from negligible. So if anyone considers them profitable, let him make use of them; anyone who does not consider them so may give them to his father to keep and attend to.

For not all things give pleasure to all men, nor do all men consider all subjects worthy of study. Although I was born later than many accomplished writers of an earlier day, the accident of date ought not to mulct me of praise, if I too produce a learned work whose ampler research and whose choice of language make it deserving of serious attention.

Mythology, mariners' yarns, vulgar superstitions, the ascertained facts of nature—all serve to adorn a tale and, on occasion, to point a moral. His religion is the popular stoicism of the age. Aleian repeatedly affirms his belief in the gods and in divine providence; the wisdom and beneficence of Nature are held up to veneration; the folly and selfishness of man are contrasted with the untaught virtues of the animal world. Some animals, to be sure, have their failings, but he chooses rather to dwell upon their good qualities, devotion, courage, self-sacrifice, gratitude. Again, animals are guided by reason, and from them we may learn contentment, control of the passions, and calm in the face of death.

Animal Peculiarity Volume 3 Part 8

By T.P Just

~~~

Get All The Books In The Series:

Animal Peculiarity Volume 1 Part [1-8]
Animal Peculiarity Volume 2 Part [1-8]
Animal Peculiarity Volume 3 Part [1-8]
<u>Just Enterprises</u>

Table of Contents

2. The Clam

Clams of the sea are of different kinds, for some of them are rough,' others perfectly smooth '; some you can crush by the mere pressure of the fingers, others you will hardly smash with a stone ; some are of a. deep black colour, others, you might compare with silver, others again are clothed in a blend of the aforesaid colours.

Their species differ and their habitats are very various, for some lie scattered in the sands of the sea-shore or rest at times in the mud, others lie low beneath the sea-moss, while others lay hold of reefs and cling to them with might and main.

In the Istrian Sea, as it is called, these Clams in summer time at the beginning of the harvesting season swim along together like a herd of cattle, floating lightly to the surface, although-up to this time they have been too heavy and weighty to float upwards, but now they are no longer so. And they avoid the South wind and flee before the North; arid, cannot endure even the East wind, but their delight is in a wave less sea and when the pleasant and gentle breezes of the; West wind blow.

And so beneath their influence they quit their burrows, with their shells still closed and fast shut, and mount up-wards from their recesses and, when the sea is wave less, swim around. And then they open their coverings and peep forth, like brides looking down from their private chambers or like rosebuds, that warmed a little, have peeped out of their flower-cups towards the suns heat.

And so little by little they; gather courage and are glad to rest quietly while waiting for the friendly breeze; and one of their coverings the Clams spread beneath them, the other they, raise, and with the latter for sail and the former for skiff they float along. And in this way they move forward when the sea is calm and the weather fine.

To see them from a distance you would say that it was a fleet of ships. If however they perceive some vessel approaching or some savage creature advancing or some monstrous fish swimming by, with one clash of their shells they fold up, sink in a mass, and are gone.

The Haemorrhous or 'Blood-Better' is a species of snake which lives and has its haunts chiefly among rocky hollows. Its body is one foot long, and its width tapers downwards from its broad head to its tail. At one time it has a -fiery hue, at another pitch-black, and on its head there bristle what look like horns. It crawls softly as it scrapes the scales of its belly along the ground, and its course; is crooked. And so it makes a gentle rustling, which shows how sluggish and how feeble it is. But when it bites it makes a puncture which immediately appears dark blue, and the victim suffers agonising pains in. his stomach, while the belly discharges copious fluid.

On the first night after, blood streams' from the nose and throat and even from the ears together, with a bile-like poison, and the bladder emits blood-stained water. Also if there are any old scars on the body they break open.

But if a female Blood-letter darts poison as it strikes, the poison mounts to the gums, blood streams copiously from the finger-nails, and the teeth are forced out from the gums.

The Tale of Conobus and Helen

This, they say, was the savage creature that Conobus, the helmsman of Menelaus, encountered in Egypt during the reign of Thonis; and when Helen realised how strong this venomous, beast was she broke its spine and extracted the poison.

But for what purpose she was eager to obtain this precious stuff I am unable to say.

3. Animals presented to the Indian King

The people of India bring to their king tigers that they have trained, tame panthers, four-horned antelopes, two kinds of oxen, the one swift of foot, the other exceedingly wild. From these oxen they contrive fly-whisks, and whereas the rest of their body is entirely black, their tails are dazzlingly white. They bring also pale-yellow doves which are said never to become domesticated, never to be tamed; those birds too which they are accustomed to call *Cercoronoi* (mynahs); and hounds of good pedigree (I have spoken of these above); and apes, some white, some the deepest black: the reddish ones, which are too fond of women, they do not introduce; into their towns, but if they can contrive somehow to spring upon them, they put them to death, because they detest them as adulterers.

4. Animal Contests in India

In India the Great King on one day in every year arranges contests not only for various creatures, as I have said elsewhere, but among them between dumb animals also, or at any rate for those which are born with horns.
And these butt each other and struggle with an instinct truly astonishing until one is victorious, as in fact athletes do, using all their strength to win the highest prizes or to achieve glorious renown and a noble fame. But these dumb combatants are wild bulls, tame rams, and what are called *mesoi* and one-horned asses and *hyainai*.
They say that this animal is smaller than a gazelle but far more spirited than a stag and that it vents its fury with its horns.
And last of all there come forward elephants to the fight: they advance and wound one another to the death with their tusks, and frequently one comes off victor and kills its adversary; frequently also both die together.

5. The viper and its young

Theophrastus denies that the young of a Viper eat through their mother's belly, as though they were breaking open a door (if I may be allowed the jest) or forcing an exit that had been blocked; but as the female is subjected to pressure and as its belly is (to use the language of Homer) straitened, it is unable to hold out and so bursts.

The Pipe-fish

And his statement convinces me, for, you see, Pipe-fish too having no womb and being slim go through the same process with their young. As I have explained somewhere earlier on. But I trust that Herodotus will not be angry with me if I reckon as fables all that he says regarding the birth, of Vipers.

6. Lion and dolphin compared

It seems that there is a certain natural association and kinship of a mysterious kind between the Spared Lion and the Dolphin. It is not merely that one is king of land-animals and the other of fishes of the sea, but that when they advance to old age and begin to waste away, the Lion takes a land-monkey by way of medicine while the Dolphin searches for its equivalent in the sea.

I have stated somewhere that the sea also contains a ' monkey' and this is beneficial to; the Dolphin, just as the land-monkey is to the Lion.

7. The Sepedon

Among the creatures which I have not described and which
are past numbering, is the *Sepedon,* an evil reptile. Nicander
says that it is the same colour as the Blood-letter and is akin to
it in appearance.

This also he says: it seems to move more quickly, but conveys
the impression of being smaller for its path is crooked and
tortuous, arid it is chiefly for this reason that it deceives the
spectator as to, its real size.

Now the wound which it inflicts is terrible: at any rate it
spreads and festers and. proves that the aforesaid creature is
true to its name. At any rate the poison forces its way over the
entire body with irresistible speed, arid what is more, the hair
turns clammy and perishes; the eyebrows and eyelashes fall
away; darkness comes over the eyes and they are covered
with white spots.

8. The Tortoise, male and female

The land-Tortoise is a most lustful creature, at least the male is; the female however mates unwillingly. And Demostratus, a member I may add, of the Roman Senate not that this makes Kim a sufficient voucher, though in my opinion he attained the summit of knowledge in matters of fishing and was an admirable expounder of his knowledge; nor should I be surprised if he had made a study of some weightier subject and had dealt with the science of the soul.

This Demostratus admits that he does not know precisely whether there is any other reason for the female declining to copulate, but he claims to vouch for the following fact. The female couples only when looking towards the male, and when he has satisfied his desire he goes away, while the female is quite unable to turn over again owing to the bulk of her shell and because she has been pressed into the ground.

And so she is abandoned by her mate to provide a meal for other animals and especially for eagles. This then, according to Demostratus, is what the females dread, and since their desires are moderate and they prefer life to pleasurable indulgence, the males are unable to coax them to the act.

And so by some mysterious instinct the males cast an amorous spell 'that brings forgetfulness of all' fear. It seems that the spells of a Tortoise in loving mood are by no means songs, like the trifles which Theocritus, the composer of sportive pastoral poems, wrote, but a mysterious herb of which Demostratus admits that neither he nor anyone else knows the name. Apparently the males adorn themselves with this herb and some mysterious. . . . At any rate if they hold this herb in their mouth there ensues the exact opposite to what I have described: the male becomes coy, but the female hitherto reluctant is now full of ardour and pursues him in a frenzied desire to mate; fear is banished and the females are not in the least afraid for their own safety.

9. The Cock in Nibas

There is a region near to Thessalonica in Macedon which goes by the name of Nibas. Now the Cocks there lack-their natural faculty of crowing and are absolutely silent.

There is current a proverbial saying applied to things that are impossible, it is to this effect: 'you shall have such-and-such when Nibas crows.

10. A Monstrous Snake

When Alexander threw some parts of India a monstrous into a
commotion and took possession of others he encountered
among many other animals a Serpent; which lived in a cavern
and was regarded as sacred by the Indians who paid it great
and superstitious reverence.

Accordingly Indians went to all lengths imploring Alexander
to permit nobody to attack the Serpent; and he assented to
their wish. Now as the army passed by the cavern arid caused
a noise the Serpent was aware of it. (It has, you know, the
sharpest hearing and the keenest sight of all animals.)

And it hissed and snorted so violently that all were terrified
and confounded. It was reported to measure 70 cubits
although it was not visible in all its length, for it only put its
head out. At any rate its eyes are said to have been the size of
a large, round Macedonian shield.

11. Crow and Eagle

Crows make it their business to worry Eagles, but they despise the Crows and leave them to fly at a lower level, while they themselves cleave the upper air on the swiftest of wings, not of course because they are afraid (how could anyone knowing well what the might of Eagles is say such a thing!): it is rather from what I may call their own magnanimity that they allow those birds to go their miserable way down below.

12. The Pilot-fish

They say that the Pilot-fish is sacred not only to Poseidon but is also beloved of the gods of Samothrace. At any rate a certain fisherman in the olden days was punished by this fish. The name of the fisherman was, according to the story, Epopeus, and he came from the island of Icarus and had a son.
Now on one occasion after they had failed to find any fish Epopeus drew up his net with a catch consisting entirely of Pilot-fish, off which' he and his son made a meal. But not long after, avenging justice overtook him, for a sea-monster attacked his boat and swallowed Epopeus before the very eyes of his son.
And they also say that Dolphins are the enemies of the Pilot-fish, and they again do not escape unharmed when they eat one, for they immediately begin to writhe and go quite mad, and being incapable of remaining still are carried on to beaches, and when once they are cast ashore by the wave they furnish a meal to sea-crows and sea-mews.

And Apollonius of Rhodes or of Naucratis says that the Pilot-fish was once actually a human being and a ferryman. And Apollo fell in love with a maiden and attempted to lie with her, but she escaped and came to Miletus and implored one Pompilus, a seaman, to conduct her across the strait. He agreed to do so, but Apollo appeared and seized the maiden, turned the ship into stone, and transformed Pompilus into this fish.

13. Horses affected by certain water

It is reported that Horses which drink from Horses the river Cossinitus (it is in Thrace) become terribly savage. This river empties itself into the territory of Abdera and is swallowed up in the Lake of the Bistones. Here, you know, was once the palace of Diomedes the Thracian who owned those famous wild mares, one of the 'Labours' of Heracles.

And they say that the same fate befalls horses that drink from the spring at Potniae. The place called Potniae, where the spring is, lies not far from Thebes. They say that the inhabitants of Oraea and Gechrosia give their Horses fish for fodder, arid I am told that the Celts feed both their cattle and their horses on fish.

In their country, it is said, the Horses actually flee from the scent of human beings and hasten to the more southerly parts of Europe, especially when the South Wind blows.

Fed on Fish

And there are those who bear witness to the fact that the inhabitants of Macedonia and of Lydia also feed fed on fish their horses on fish, and who assert that the sheep of Lydia and of Macedonia are fattened on the same diet.

14. Affected by music

In Moesia while Mares are in process of being covered some people play the pipe, accompanying the marriage of Horses with nuptial music, as it affected by were; and the Mares are so enchanted by the melody that they very soon become pregnant and, what is more, produce beautiful foals.
This too I have heard concerning Horses. They say that when Horses are older and advanced in years the offspring which they beget is feeble, having besides other defects poor legs. The age and life of Horses men their age reckon as so many years: in the case of Stallions, five and thirty. But Aristotle the son of Nicomachus states that a Horse lived for five and severity years.

15. Scorpions in Persia

In the second stage of a journey from Susa in Persia to Media there are said to be Scorpions in multitudes, so that when the Persian King is going to pass that way he issues orders three days in advance that everybody is to hunt them, and bestows presents on the man who has caught the greatest number.
For if this were not done, the region would be impassable, for 'beneath every stone ' and every clod 'there lurks a scorpion.' And they say that the inhabitants of Rhoeteum were driven out by centipedes, so great was the multitude that invaded them.

16. The Acomys

They say too that in Cyrene there are species of mice which differ not only in colour but in form: some for instance have fiat-faces like martens, others again look like hedgehogs (*echinot*), and these natives call prickly mice' *(eckinees)*.

The Jeroba
And I have heard that in Egypt there are mice. The Jerboa with only two legs, and that they grow to a great size, but their front legs they use as hands, for they are shorter than their hind legs. And they walk erect on their two legs, but when pursued they jump. This is what Theophrastus says

17. The Francolins

There is a story that the birds known as Francolins when transported from Lydia to Egypt and let loose in the woods, at first uttered the note of a quail. Later on, owing to the river being confined in its hollow bed, a famine broke out and many of the inhabitants perished, whereupon these same birds' never ceased to utter with a sound far clearer and more articulate than any child words meaning ' Three curses on the accursed.

And the same story tells how if they are captured and snared they not only refuse to be tamed but no longer even utter the notes which they did before: their servitude and confinement decree silence against them.

If however they are. Let go and can unfold their wings at liberty and return to their own haunts, they again become vocal and recover both their voice and their freedom of speech together.

18. The Little Horned Owl

They say that men catch the Little Horned Owl also (mentioned in the *Odyssey* by Homer who says that it nests in great numbers round about the cavern of Calypso) by dancing. And dancers assert that a certain kind of dance is called after this bird, and if we are to believe them this dance has been called 'the Little Horned Owl.

And that anyone should caricature and imitate them in a playful way affords these birds the greatest pleasure. This is the origin of the word *skoptein* which we use, meaning 'to mock.' It is said that the Little Horned Owl is smaller than the Little Owl and that its colour resembles lead of the deepest hue, but, its wings are said to have whitish speckles.

And it displays two feathers rising from the brows on either temple. Callimachus maintains that there are two kinds of Little Horned Owl, one kind is vocal, the other doomed to silence; the latter is called *skops*, the former *aeiskops*. But Aristotle asserts that in Homer the word does not begin with a *sigma (skops)*, but that the birds are called simply *hopes*.

So those who prefix a *sigma* mistake the true spelling of the word and are mistaken as to Homer's judgment and knowledge of the bird.

At all other seasons of the year the Little Horned Owl is not edible, but only when caught on one or two days in the late autumn, and then it is edible. These *Skopes* differ from the *Aeiskopes* in bulk, and bear some resemblance to a turtle-dove or a ring-dove.

19. The Pygmies

As to the race of Pygmies I have heard that The they are governed in a manner peculiar to themselves, and that in fact owing to the failure of the male line a certain woman became queen and ruled over the Pygmies.

And their Queen

Her name was Gerana, and the Pygmies worshipped her as a god, paying her honours too august for a human being. The result was, they say, that she became so puffed up in her mind that she held the goddesses of no account. It was especially Hera, Athena, Artemis, and Aphrodite that, she said, came nowhere near her in beauty. But she was not destined to escape the evil consequences of her diseased imagination. For in consequence of the anger of Hera she changed her original form into that of a most hideous bird and became the crane of today and wages war on the Pygmies because with their excessive honours they drove her to madness and to her destruction.

Get All The Books In The Series:

Animal Peculiarity Volume 1 Part [1-8]
Animal Peculiarity Volume 2 Part [1-8]
Animal Peculiarity Volume 3 Part [1-8]